Baseball Game (Berkeley Boys Books)

Set 7 - Book 1

Berkeley Boys Books

Caleb Berkeley
(Bestselling Author,
Creator of over 55 books)

Elisha Berkeley
(Creator of over 35 books)

Caleb and Elisha Berkeley

Baseball game (Berkeley Boys Books)

By: Caleb and Elisha Berkeley

Print ISBN: 978-1-989612-80-4

Published by C.M. Berkeley Media Group

www.cmberkeleymediagroup.com

Copyright© 2022 by Caleb and Elisha Berkeley. All rights reserved.

Without limiting the rights under copyright reserved above, no part of this publication may be reproduced, stored in or introduced into a retrieval system, or transmitted, in any form, or by any means (electronic, mechanical, photocopying, recording, or otherwise) without the prior written permission of both the copyright owner and the above publisher of this book. Any resemblance to characters, places, brands, media, and incidents are purely coincidental. The author acknowledges the trademarked status and trademark owners of various products referenced in this work, which have been used without permission. The publication/use of these trademarks is not authorized, associated with, or sponsored by the trademark owners.

Digital Edition License Notes

The digital version of this book is licensed for your individual personal enjoyment only. This digital book may not be re-sold or given away to other people. If you would like to share this book with another person, please purchase an additional copy for each person you share it with. If you're reading this book and did not purchase it, or it was not purchased for your use only, then you should return to your online e-book retailer or the author's website and purchase your own copy. Thank you for respecting the author's work.

Baseball Game (Berkeley Boys Books)
Other Great Books

Grab these titles at Amazon, Barnes and Noble and other major online book sellers.

Caleb and Elisha Berkeley
Other Great Books

Get them all at major online book sellers today!

Baseball Game (Berkeley Boys Books)

Other Great Books

Grab these titles at Amazon, Barnes and Noble and other major online book sellers.

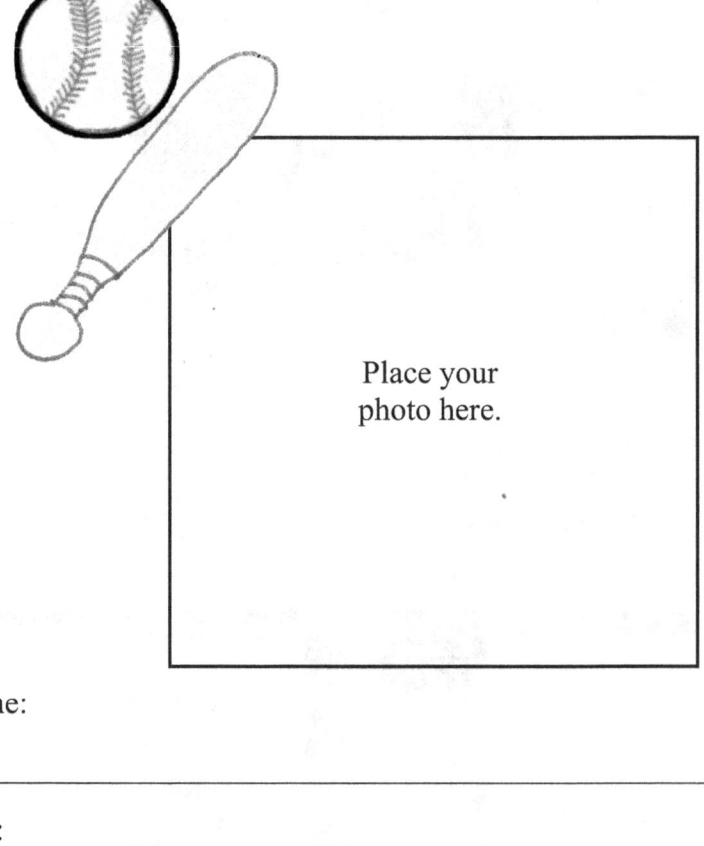

Place your photo here.

Name:

Age:

City:

This is Billy

Caleb and Elisha Berkeley

> Baseball game takes place on June 8th

There's a baseball game

Billy and his dad goes to the game

Billy grabs his bat

His friend throws the baseball

Billy hits the baseball

Billy runs

Caleb and Elisha Berkeley

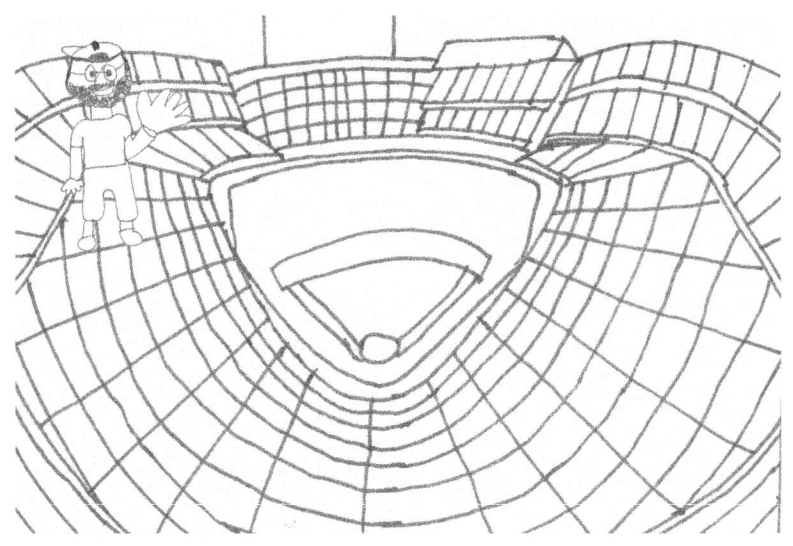

His dad cheers

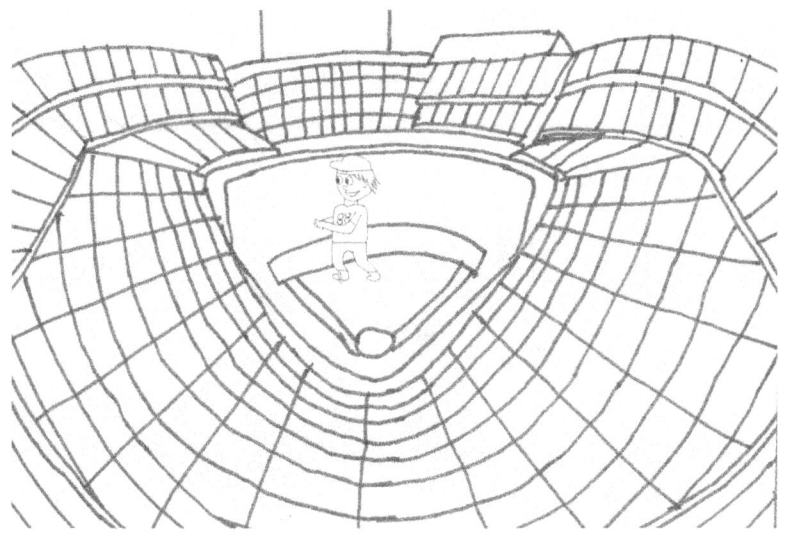

Billy scores a run

Their team won

The End

Caleb and Elisha Berkeley

New words we learned today!

1. Baseball
2. Friend
3. Throws
4. Hits
5. Runs
6. Cheer
7. Game
8. Dad
9. Team
10. Grabs
11. Bat
12. Score

It's time for a MAZE!!

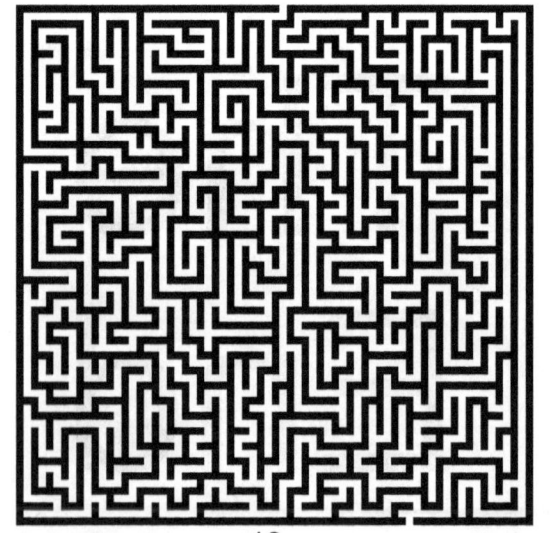

Baseball Game (Berkeley Boys Books)

Word Scrambles

EBAALBLS _ _ _ _ _ _ _ _

EGAM _ _ _ _

DDA _ _ _

EMTA _ _ _ _

BRASG _ _ _ _ _

ATB _ _ _

REIDFN _ _ _ _ _ _

WSRHTO _ _ _ _ _ _ _

SHIT _ _ _ _

UNSR _ _ _ _

REHCE _ _ _ _ _

ORESC _ _ _ _ _

19

Caleb and Elisha Berkeley

Word Searches

F	P	S	W	W	T	F	H	G	S	U	T	K	K	Q
K	N	G	U	Q	T	Y	M	V	S	Q	W	W	W	G
J	K	B	L	W	H	B	A	S	E	B	A	L	L	T
X	X	A	T	F	R	R	M	R	U	U	H	G	H	W
I	L	X	V	W	O	U	H	Z	F	G	Q	J	I	N
W	N	O	W	W	W	N	D	T	E	R	H	X	T	C
E	B	L	X	D	S	S	E	V	N	J	I	O	S	P
D	X	K	A	H	G	A	L	E	W	X	Z	E	H	Z
O	L	D	C	P	M	P	N	S	K	T	A	F	N	G
S	M	O	Q	B	L	G	P	C	C	E	S	T	E	D
R	B	W	J	A	Q	T	W	L	T	C	B	M	B	D
E	F	B	E	T	T	M	T	S	Q	R	A	T	Y	J
E	H	W	N	S	C	O	R	E	P	G	R	X	P	S
H	B	K	V	R	W	R	H	C	G	L	G	N	G	H
C	A	M	C	H	H	X	B	I	O	R	E	W	S	D

BASEBALL   GAME   TEAM
BAT   GRABS   THROWS
CHEERS   HITS
DAD   RUNS
FRIEND   SCORE

Baseball Game (Berkeley Boys Books)

About Caleb Berkeley

Caleb Berkeley is a published author since he was 7 years old. He is a product of the Montessori school. At 16, he's a veteran storyteller and creator of the popular children's book series, The Adventures of Moshe Monkey and Elias Froggy. Caleb is the creator of over 50 books with more coming soon. Caleb created puzzle books, easy reader books, planners, journals, writing books, and learning books for kids. Caleb is also a videographer, and video editor and the co-founder of the BerkeleyChefs channel. The BerkeleyChefs channel is a plant-based channel that was created to help parents and kids have fun cooking healthy meals together. You can check the channel on: berkeleychefs.com. Caleb is also a game card creator and an accomplished self-taught painter whose artwork has been featured at a local art gallery and the Whitby Public Library. He has sold a few of his

original pieces and you can buy prints or originals for your family at: berkeleyfamilyart.com. Caleb likes to learn new stuff and do gardening in his spare time.

About Elisha Berkeley

Elisha Berkeley is an author following his brother. His first book was published at the age of 7. At the age of 12, Elisha's been working hard to create helpful books for kids. Elisha is currently an author of over 30 books. Elisha created easy reader books, a planner, writing books, and learning books for kids. Elisha is also the co-founder of the BerkeleyChefs channel along with his brother Caleb. You can check the channel on: berkeleychefs.com. Elisha is also an accomplished self- taught painter whose artwork was also featured in a local art gallery and in the Whitby Public Library. His original art pieces as well as prints are available for your family to enjoy. He has sold a few of his original pieces and you can buy prints or originals for your family at:

berkeleyfamilyart.com. In his spare time, Elisha likes to make smackalicious foods, and spend time outdoors.

Baseball Game (Berkeley Boys Books)
Answers to the Puzzles

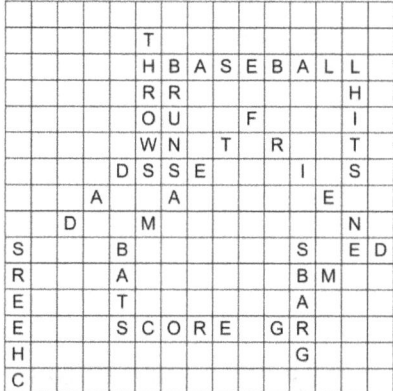

EBAALBLS = BASEBALL

EGAM = GAME

DDA = DAD

EMTA = TEAM

BRASG = GRABS

ATB = BAT

REIDFN = FRIEND

WSRHTO = THROWS

SHIT = HITS

UNSR = RUNS

REHCE = CHEER

ORESC = SCORE

Grab the rest of set 5 today at major online bookstores

Caleb and Elisha Berkeley
More from CM Berkeley Media Group

CM Berkeley Media Group, based in Canada, works with its authors to produce books which help to uplift the human spirit, spread the message of health and wellness, and offer practical insights in finances, and other areas.

Website: cmberkeleymediagroup.com

Grab these other great titles at Amazon worldwide and other major online booksellers.

For Adults
- Break The Poverty Curse: Unlock Your Prosperity 2022 & 2023 Success Planner - School of Prophets Edition
  (A Great tool for 17 to 70. This contains more information to help structure your life spiritually and in this life.
- Break The Poverty Curse: Unlock Your Prosperity (2017 Edition)
- Break The Poverty Curse: Unlock Your Prosperity 2019 Success Planner
  (A Great tool for 10 to adults. Learn basic necessary life planning skills)
- Break The Poverty Curse: Unlock Your Prosperity 2019 Success Planner - ULTIMATE Edition
  (A Great tool for 17 to adults. This contains more information to help structure your progress)
- Break The Poverty Curse: Unlock Your Prosperity 2019 Success Planner - WRITER'S Edition
  (A great tool for 17 to adults who have dreams of becoming an author. Use this planner to write your book in under a year)
- Break The Poverty Curse: Unlock Your Prosperity - Puzzle Power 1
- Break The Poverty Curse: Unlock Your Prosperity - Puzzle Power 2
- Break The Poverty Curse: Unlock Your Prosperity - Puzzle Power 3

- Break The Poverty Curse: Unlock Your Prosperity - CRASH PROOF (coming soon)

Baseball Game (Berkeley Boys Books)
Jenny's 99 Health Quotes To Empower Your Life

Eating4Eternity: Unlock Your Holistic Health Lifestyle. Sweet Raw Desserts: Life Is Sweet Raw™

Can I Offer You A Cigarette: The Only Sure Way To Break The Smoking Habit

Colon By Design: Overcoming The Stigma Of Colon Sickness And Unlocking True Colon Health™

Fresh Food4Life™: The Case For Taking Back Control of Your Food And Empowering Your Family And Community.

For Teens and Young Adults

The Youth Leadership Empowerment System™

Jump into the world of Dr Vicktor Maximitas, world famous psychologist by day and legendary demon hunter by night. Go into this mystery world where good triumphs over evil and souls are rescued from demonic clutches. This is a new series by Vaughn Berkeley.
- A Maximitas Novel: Unholy Fyre (Book 1)
- A Maximitas Novel: Unholy Fyre (Book 2)
- A Maximitas Novel: Unholy Fyre (Book 3)

For Children

The Adventures of Moshe Monkey and Elias Froggy book series.
- The Adventures of Moshe Monkey and Elias Froggy: A Healthy Business (Volume 1)
- Moshe and Elias Build A Garden (The Adventures of Moshe Monkey and Elias Froggy) (Volume 2)
- Moshe and Elias Tropical Vacation (The Adventures of Moshe Monkey and Elias Froggy) (Volume 3)
- Living Foods for Boys and Girls (The Adventures of Moshe Monkey and Elias Froggy) (Volume 4)
- Moshe Monkey Breaks His Leg (The Adventures of Moshe Monkey and Elias Froggy) (Volume 5)
- Moshe And Elias 2019 Daily Success Planner
- Moshe Monkey And Elias Froggy 2019-2020 Back to

Caleb and Elisha Berkeley

School Success Planner
- Moshe Monkey And Elias Froggy: Puzzle Book (1 to 9)
- Fun with your ABC's
- The Amazing Colouring and Learning Book of Fruits and Veggies
- 2020 Biblical Planner
- School of the Prophets for Children Planner - Ultimate Edition
- Moshe Monkey And Elias Froggy - Daily Journal
- Baldy's Life
- Baldy's Writing Book for New Words
- Berkeley Short Stories, Doodles and Writing Prompts
- Scripture Brain Power 1
- Scripture Brain Power 2
- Roll the Ball
- Mom and Dad
- Ann Can Count To 10
- My Easy Cursive Handwriting Book
- Bounce the Ball
- Mow the Lawn
- Mouzzie Goes Home (Mouzzie Mouse Adventures) (Book 1)

* * * * *

Check out these titles on Amazon and major online book sellers.

Baseball Game (Berkeley Boys Books)
Great Resources

Berkeley Chefs (berkeleychefs.com)
The Berkeley Chefs channel is where parents can find videos and recipes on how to cook healthy, delicious, plant-based meals with there kids.

Berkeley Family Art (berkeleyfamilyart.com)
This site showcases the original artwork by members of the Berkeley Family. You can order originals and prints from this site.

VaughnBerkeley.com
Vaughn's site for those on a spiritual journey to get closer to our God and creator.

CM Berkeley Media Group (cmberkeleymediagroup.com)
CM Berkeley Media Group is the digital media company founded by Vaughn Berkeley. The company publishes books that have a message to uplift individuals. There are books for children, teens, and adults.

The Book on Quantum Website
www.thebookonquantum.com
This is the website to find all the information on current books and upcoming books in the series, "The Book on Quantum", by Vaughn Berkeley.

EternityWatch Magazine
(www.eternitywatchmagazine.com)
Great site for vegan, raw-vegan, and holistic health and wellness information.

Eating4Eternity.org (www.eating4eternity.org)
Eating4Eternity is founded by Jenny Berkeley and is focused on her personal coaching approach. On the site, you will find news articles on health and wellness.

Berkeley Academy (http://berkeley.academy)
This is the online educational institute founded by Vaughn Berkeley and carrying on the tradition and heritage of the Berkeley name and role in educating the masses. Vaughn's passion has been education from as long as he can remember.

www.ingramcontent.com/pod-product-compliance
Lightning Source LLC
Chambersburg PA
CBHW070051070426
42449CB00012BA/3227